American Lives

Anne Hutchinson

Elizabeth Raum

Heinemann Library
Chicago, Illinois

© 2005 Heinemann Library
a division of Reed Elsevier Inc.
Chicago, Illinois

Customer Service 888-454-2279
Visit our website at www.heinemannlibrary.com

Designed by Heinemann Library
Photo research by Jill Birschbach
Printed and bound in China by WKT Company
Limited

09 08 07 06 05
10 9 8 7 6 5 4 3 2 1

Library of Congress Cataloging-in-Publication Data
Raum, Elizabeth.
    Anne Hutchinson / by Elizabeth Raum.
        p. cm. -- (American lives)
    Includes bibliographical references and index.
    ISBN 1-4034-5958-4 (HC), 1-4034-5966-5 (Pbk.)
    1. Hutchinson, Anne Marbury, 1591-1643--
Juvenile literature. 2. Puritan women--
Massachusetts--Biography--Juvenile literature. 3.
Puritans--Massachusetts--Biography--Juvenile
literature. 4. Massachusetts--History--Colonial
period, ca. 1600-1775--Juvenile literature. 5.
Puritans--Massachusetts--History--17th century--
Juvenile literature. [1. Hutchinson, Anne Marbury,
1591-1643. 2. Puritans. 3. Massachusetts--History--
Colonial period, ca. 1600-1775. 4. Women--
Biography.] I. Title. II. Series: American lives
(Heinemann Library (Firm))
    F67.H92R38 2004
    973.2'2'092--dc22

                         2003027784

Acknowledgments
The author and publishers are grateful to the
following for permission to reproduce copyright
material:

Cover photograph by Bettmann/Corbis

Title page, pp. 5, 11, 13, 16, 18, 20, 21, 23, 25, 26,
28 Bettmann/Corbis; pp. 4, 6, 8 Mary Evans Picture
Library; p. 7 The Bridgeman Art Library; p. 10
Bryan Pickering/Eye Ubiquitous/Corbis; pp. 12, 14
Hulton Archive/Getty Images; pp. 15, 19, 22, 27
North Wind Picture Archives; p. 17 Archivo
Iconografic, S. A./Corbis; p. 29 Kevin
Fleming/Corbis

The author would like to thank her husband,
Richard, for his continued support and
encouragement.

The publisher would like to thank Michelle Rimsa
for her comments in the preparation of this book.

For more information about the image of Anne
Hutchinson that appears on the cover of this book,
turn to page 5.

Contents

Some words are shown in bold, **like this.** You can find out what they mean by looking in the glossary.

Childhood

When Anne Hutchinson was a child, most girls did not go to school. Anne was different. Her father taught her reading, writing, and religion. Anne's father believed that girls were as smart as boys. Anne learned quickly. Her father was pleased when Anne asked questions and came up with her own ideas. He believed that women could be leaders in the church and the community. When Anne grew up, she proved him right.

This picture shows a typical view of English village life in the 1600s. Anne grew up in a village a lot like this one.

This drawing shows Anne wearing the type of clothes that most women wore during the 1600s.

Anne Marbury was born in Alford, England, in July 1591. Anne was the second of thirteen children born to Francis Marbury and his wife, Bridget Dryden. As the oldest daughter, Anne helped her mother to take care of the younger children. Anne's mother, who was a **midwife,** taught Anne how to help women during childbirth and how to make medicines from plants and **herbs.**

London

In 1605, when Anne was fourteen, her father took a job as a **minister** at a church in London. It took the Marburys ten days to travel 125 miles (201 kilometers) from Alford to London. Anne liked the city. She met people with new ideas. Anne learned to question their ideas and to say what she believed.

This drawing shows what London, England, looked like around the time Anne and her family moved there.

This English illustration from the 1600s is meant to show the ideal, happy marriage.

When Anne was nineteen, her father died. Anne moved with her mother and younger brothers and sisters to another home in London. She helped her mother care for the large family. One day Anne met William Hutchinson. William and Anne had been friends when they were children in Alford. William had come to London for work. Anne and William fell in love. On August 9, 1612, they were married.

Family

William and Anne moved back to Alford. William was a sheep farmer and **merchant.** He sold **textiles,** or fabrics. Anne's father had left her some money, so the young couple purchased a large home with a stable. The home had many bedrooms that the Hutchinsons soon filled with children. Their first child, Edward, was born in May 1613. Over time, they had fifteen children.

Many couples in the 1600s farmed their land, as seen above. Since William and Anne had a stable, raking hay was probably a common chore for them.

William and Anne sometimes traveled to nearby towns to go to religious meetings.

Time spent in England

Although many children died in childhood during the 1600s, Anne's children were very healthy. Like her mother, Anne was a **midwife** who helped women during childbirth and prepared medicines to help neighbors. William's business did well. He became a town leader.

There was no **minister** at the church in Alford. When Anne and William heard about a new minister at St. Botolph's Church in Boston, England, 24 miles (39 kilometers) from Alford, they went to hear him.

9

John Cotton

The Hutchinsons liked the Reverend John Cotton, who was a **Puritan.** The Puritans were a group that wanted to change the king's church, the **Church of England.** Cotton preached that it was by faith in God, not by holy actions or formal ceremonies, that people got into heaven.

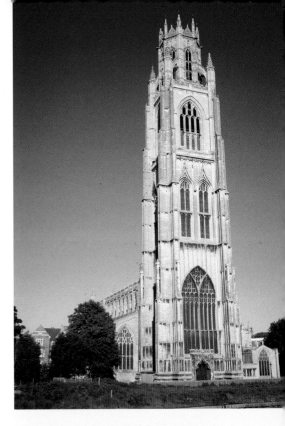

Anne traveled many miles to St. Botolph's Church to hear John Cotton preach.

Anne Hutchinson agreed with John Cotton's new ideas. However, the new King of England, Charles I, disagreed. He believed that people had to earn God's love by following the laws and doing good deeds. People began fighting over these ideas.

The Life of Anne Hutchinson

1591	1612	1634	1637
Born in Alford, England	Married William Hutchinson	Left for Massachusetts	Brought to trial

The Hutchinsons went to Boston several times a year to hear John Cotton preach. They traveled a day and a half to reach Boston. They stayed four or five days. Cotton preached six times a week, and Anne went to every service while she was in town. She considered John Cotton her teacher.

When she returned to Alford, she held meetings in her home to discuss Cotton's **sermons.** She also taught Bible lessons. Many people, both men and women, attended. Anne was a good teacher.

John Cotton was an important Puritan minister in Boston, England.

1638	**1638**	**1642**	**1643**
Banished from Massachusetts; joined Roger William's colony in Rhode Island	*Founded Portsmouth, Rhode Island, with her followers*	*Husband William died*	*Killed in a Native American attack*

The New World

King Charles began arresting **Puritans** like John Cotton. Many Puritans sailed to the New World. The Hutchinsons considered going with them. However, Anne had just given birth to her daughter Katherine. It was too soon for the baby to travel. In 1630 two of Anne's daughters, sixteen-year-old Susanna and eight-year-old Elizabeth, died. When John Cotton left for North America in 1633, the Hutchinsons decided to take the same ship the next year.

King Charles I ruled England from 1625 to 1649.

This picture shows Puritans leaving for North America. Many people left their homelands for religious reasons.

Anne, William, and ten of their children boarded a ship called the *Griffin* in 1634. The ship was crowded. For two months, 100 passengers, 50 crew, and 100 cattle were on the ship, crossing the Atlantic Ocean. The passengers were often seasick.

Anne visited with the women on board. She talked with them about religion and John Cotton's new ideas. The women liked her, but some of the men on the ship were upset that a woman was acting like a **minister** and teaching religion.

Boston

Many ships like the one pictured here brought people to North America in the 1600s.

On September 18, 1634, the *Griffon* landed in Boston, Massachusetts. One of the passengers, the Reverend Zechariah Symmes, went directly to Boston church leaders to tell them that Anne was teaching about God and the Bible. He did not approve of a woman teaching about religion. When Anne and William applied to become members of the Boston church, William was accepted right away, but Anne was not.

Church leaders questioned Anne about her beliefs. After a week, they allowed her to join the church where John Cotton was a teacher. Anne attended worship services on Sundays.

Many women gathered in homes for afternoon prayer meetings led by men. Anne was too busy caring for her large family to join them. Anne spent her days cooking, cleaning, and washing. She continued to help deliver babies and to make medicines out of the **herbs** she grew in her garden.

Puritans spent much of their time at religious meetings.

Meetings

The church in Boston was very **strict.** A friend warned Anne Hutchinson that she should attend the small-group meetings. Going to church was not enough. So Hutchinson decided to hold meetings for women in her own home like she had done in Alford. Only five or six women attended the first meeting, but about 60 showed up for the second one. They came because they realized that Hutchinson was a good leader who knew a great deal about religion.

Aside from going to church, colonial women were expected to cook, clean, and take care of their children.

Sir Henry Vane became governor of Massachusetts in 1636.

Soon Hutchinson held two meetings a week. She tried to explain John Cotton's sermons. She taught that a person goes to heaven because of faith in God, not because of doing good things. Almost all the women in Boston attended Hutchinson's meetings. Several men began to join the meetings, too. Even the new governor, Henry Vane, attended. Hutchinson, who was an excellent teacher, was not afraid to speak to them all.

Speaking Out

Hutchinson started sharing her own ideas. She **criticized** the church leaders who did not agree with her. She said which **ministers** were good and which were not.

The church leaders, especially John Winthrop, became upset with her. The ministers were even more upset when Hutchinson and her followers left church during a **sermon** they did not like.

This painting shows a group of Puritans walking to church.

This image shows Boston and its harbor in the 1600s.

John Winthrop, the first governor of Massachusetts, lived across the street from the Hutchinsons. He watched all the people coming and going from the Hutchinson house. He was afraid that if people believed Hutchinson's teaching that good behavior was not as important as faith in God, they would stop obeying the laws of Boston.

John Cotton warned her to be quiet, but Hutchinson refused. She was not afraid to speak up for what she believed.

Trouble

A Puritan service included reading from the Bible.
Leaders did not like Hutchinson teaching on her own.

The people in the Massachusetts Bay Colony needed the cloth and other supplies that William Hutchinson sold. His business did well, and he became a city leader. The people of Boston liked the Hutchinsons. But life for William, Anne, and their children was about to change.

In a May 1637 election, Governor Vane was **defeated.** John Winthrop became governor again. He decided to stop Anne Hutchinson's religious meetings.

Governor Winthrop called a meeting of all the **ministers** from Massachusetts and Connecticut. They wrote a list of 82 ideas that they called **heresies,** or teachings not in line with the church. They would not allow these ideas in the church. Hutchinson read the list. Several of the ideas were ones she believed in. She kept right on teaching them.

It did not take the governor long to call Hutchinson to appear in court. If she were judged **guilty,** she would be **banished,** or forced to leave Massachusetts forever.

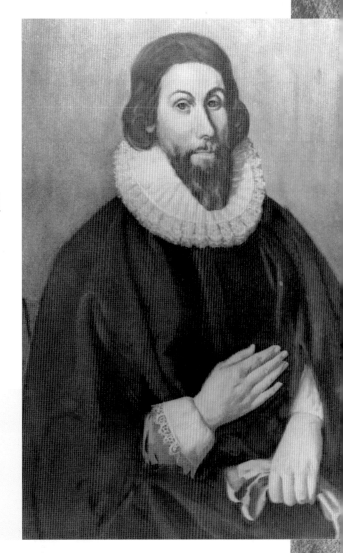

Governor John Winthrop led the Massachusetts Bay Colony that settled in the Massachusetts area.

Trial

The Hutchinsons knew that Anne might be **banished.** Anne, who was expecting another baby, bravely headed to court in November 1637.

Governor John Winthrop and the other ministers of Massachusetts were the judges. Winthrop accused Hutchinson of causing trouble in the churches. They expected Hutchinson to be quiet and listen, but she asked what **charge** had been brought against her.

This image shows a typical Massachusetts courtroom in the 1600s.

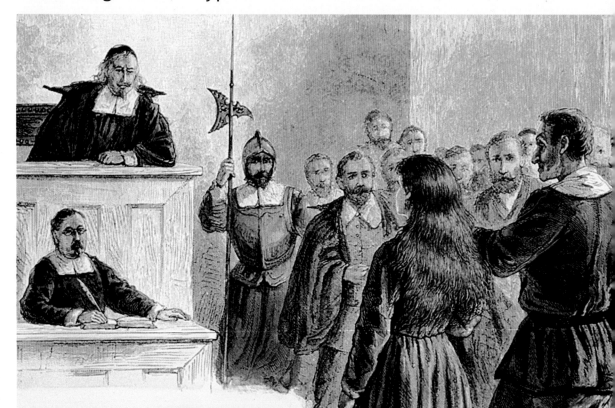

This picture shows Hutchinson standing up to church leaders during her trial.

Governor Winthrop told her that only men should be teaching religion. Hutchinson quoted a Bible verse that instructed older women to teach younger women. Hutchinson insisted that there was nothing wrong with her meetings. The ministers argued that men attended the meetings, too. Hutchinson stood up for her right to hold meetings. Finally, John Cotton spoke in her support. For a while it looked as if she might go free.

Sent Away

If Hutchinson had kept quiet after Cotton spoke, she might have been allowed to stay in Massachusetts. At the last minute, though, she said that God spoke directly to her. The Boston **ministers** did not believe her. The judges **banished** Hutchinson from Massachusetts forever.

Finding a place to stay

Hutchinson had made her home in Massachusetts before church leaders forced her to leave.

Hutchinson spent the winter locked up in the home of one of the ministers. In March the church leaders called her before the judges again. They gave her one more chance to stay in Massachusetts.

She spent a week in John Cotton's home. But she would not change her views. The ministers told her she could never again join a Boston church. It was a terrible blow.

In the picture below, Hutchinson is telling the ministers that she has still not changed her views.

Rhode Island

In March 1638 Hutchinson left for Rhode Island, where people had freedom to worship as they pleased. Roger Williams had founded Rhode Island in 1636 when he had been **banished** from Boston.

Williams welcomed Hutchinson and her followers. With his help, the Hutchinsons and their followers purchased Aquidneck Island from the Narrangansett Indians. They paid with white beads, coats, and hoes.

Roger Williams was known for his good relationships with local Native American groups.

Hutchinson **founded** the town of Portsmouth, Rhode Island. It was a farming community about a day's walk from Providence. In Portsmouth, Hutchinson was free to speak about her new ideas. Her happiness ended when her husband, William, became ill and died in the spring of 1642.

This map shows the colony of Rhode Island around the year 1660.

Attacked

This painting shows the terrible attack in which Hutchinson and her five children were killed.

Hutchinson heard **rumors** that Rhode Island might join the Massachusetts Bay Colony. She did not want to deal with Governor Winthrop again. She, her six youngest children, and several other families packed up and moved to an unsettled, wooded area that is now part of New York City. Her older children stayed in Rhode Island or Boston, or returned to England.

Hutchinson had always been friendly with the Native Americans living near her. But she and her family were attacked during a war between Native Americans and nearby Dutch settlers. Only one child survived.

Today people remember Anne Hutchinson as a woman of courage, intelligence, and faith. She challenged the religious thinking of her day and fought for the freedom to speak freely. She proved that women could be intelligent and **courageous** leaders.

This sculpture of Hutchinson stands at the Massachusetts State House.

Susanna Hutchinson

*Ten-year-old Susanna Hutchinson was out picking berries when her family was attacked. She was taken captive and lived for four years among the Native Americans. After a while, family friends in New England paid a **ransom** so she could return to Rhode Island.*

Glossary

banished   sent out of a town or country

charge   reason a person is brought to trial

Church of England   national church in England

courageous   brave

criticize   find fault with

defeated   lost

found   to begin something, such as starting a colony

guilty   deserving punishment

herb   plant used as medicine

heresy   something that goes against the teachings of a church

merchant   businessman

midwife   person who helps women give birth

minister   religious leader

Puritans   group who wanted to change the Church of England

ransom   money demanded for release of a captive

rumor   unproven story, or gossip

sermon   religious speech

strict   insisting that people follow rules

textiles   cloth or fabric

More Books to Read

Clark, Beth. *Anne Hutchinson*. Mankato, Minn.: Chelsea House, 2000.

Raum, Elizabeth. *Roger Williams*. Chicago: Heinemann Library, 2005.

An older reader can help you with this book:
Mangal, Melina. *Anne Hutchinson*. Mankato, Minn.: Chelsea House, 2004.

Places to Visit

Providence Children's Museum
"Coming to Rhode Island" Display
100 South Street
Providence, Rhode Island
Visitor Information: (401) 273-KIDS

Roger Williams National Memorial
282 North Main Street
Providence, Rhode Island 02903
Visitor Information: (401) 521-7266

Index